You and the Sunshine,

DYLAN

The Life and Times of a Caring Friend

You and the Sunshine,

DYLAN

The Life and Times of a Caring Friend

Linda Sanders

Printed in the United States of America

ISBN 979-8-89114-128-5 (hc)
ISBN 979-8-89114-127-8 (sc)
ISBN 979-8-89114-129-2 (e)

Library of Congress Control Number: 2024921821

2025.03.03

MainSpring Books
5901 W. Century Blvd
Suite 750
Los Angeles, CA, US, 90045

www.mainspringbooks.com

Contents

Betty and Dylan in Conversation

Prologue   vii
Dedication   ix
Acknowledgements   xi
Foreword   xiii

Chapter One   INTRODUCTION   1
   Dylan's Story   1

Chapter Two   A LITTLE HISTORY   6
   Puppyhood   7

Chapter Three   LIFEWORK   13
   Therapeutic Work   13
   Holidays and Ceremonies   30
   Public Service   35
   Community Service   38
   Retirement   47

Chapter Four   OFF DUTY   50
   Travel and Sight Seeing   50
   Hanging with Friends   55
   Community Theater   57

Chapter Five   SUNSHINE in DOG FORM   59
    Growing Old   59
    Time to say Goodbye   61
    Summary   64
Epilogue   67

Prologue

I'm going to tell you a love story. It's definitely not x-rated. This story isn't even the mushy kind of love story. It is about a truly devoted dog named Dylan and the love he spread to young and old, male and female, black, white, red, and yellow. Dylan didn't care what flavor human you were. Nor did he need any doggie treats to give you a hug or hold your hand. He didn't even require that you speak English or any other recognizable language to listen to your story. The fact that you existed, liked dogs, and were not allergic to them were the only criteria he had in order for him to offer his unconditional healing love to you.

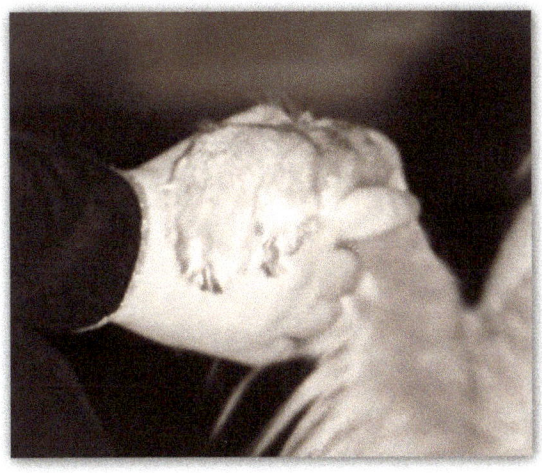

I started to write this book in 1996, a little more than 25 years ago now. I packed the draft away in 2001 due to Dylan's and my beyond-busy schedules. The draft would have most likely remained on the shelf had I not noticed warm reactions by a couple of people after they viewed old photos of Dylan. They commented about how special they were and appeared to be touched by them these many years later.

So I pulled out the old draft, changed the references to past tense, updated the narrative where it left off and added some photos. I want to apologize up front for anthropomorphizing throughout this book. I found it was the best way for me to convey what appeared to be Dylan's experiences.

My hope is that Dylan's story reminds you of what is most important in this life that we share.

Dedication

This book is dedicated to all those brave people who find themselves facing pain, fears, or are alone in the final stages of their lives, yet opened their hearts to the love of a devoted friend.

Just as Christopher Robin did, we humbly lay this book at your paws, ummm. . . feet.

"I feel better now that you're here, Dylan."

Acknowledgements

I would like to thank all the devoted healthcare professionals who can't seem to remain detached from their patients. Thank you for caring day in and day out, not just when it's convenient or when you happen to be on duty. I hope Dylan made your days a little lighter, too.

Dylan at the nurses station on Halloween.

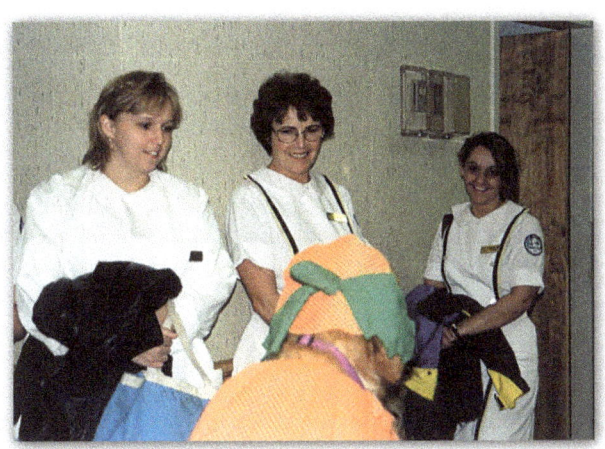

Foreword

I would like you to meet Dylan. My name is Dondi and I was Dylan's tailor. When he needed adjustments to his cape or alterations on his pumpkin costume, he came to see me. He had to be the most cooperative client I had. Besides sewing, I also worked in the Ashby Town Hall where Dylan became the official Town Hall Dog in July, 1997. Every morning when Dylan came to work with our Town Administrator, Linda, I heard his nails click on the old wood floors and his tags jingle on his collar as he trotted down the hall to see me for his good morning dog biscuit and back rub. I scratched his head and he gave me hugs. A day without Dylan was not complete.

The really wonderful thing about Dylan was that whenever I needed him, he magically appeared. It seemed to be something in the air. The first time I met him was just after my family had suffered

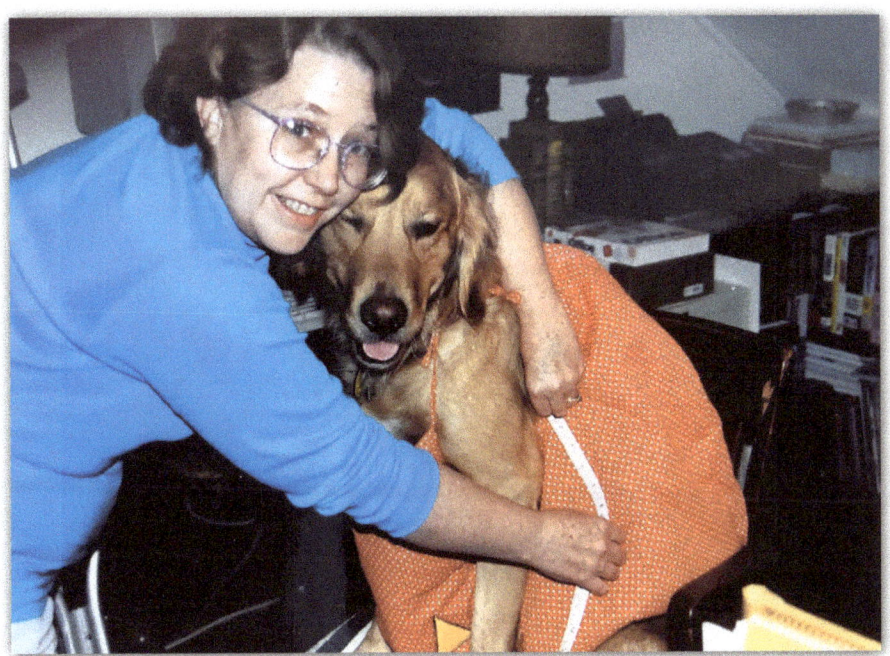

"It's okay as long as I'm able to walk in it."

the devastating loss of our nephew, Keith, to pneumonia. I, with everyone else, was reeling from the shock. There seemed to be no rest from the pain. I had never heard of a therapy dog, let alone met one. I ran into Linda and Dylan outside of our little market in Ashby. Dylan gave me a hug. He gave me a paw. He gave me a long look that wasn't in the least bit afraid of my grief. Color and warmth seemed to come back to my life right there in the street. I suddenly felt that someday I would heal. Dylan was the catalyst. No human being could have done it better.

Since our introduction at the Ashby Market, Dylan has popped up a number of times when I least expected him and most needed him. I think he was everybody's friend. Dylan had a way of making each of us who met him feel accepted without any judgments about who we were or what we were thinking or how we were feeling. He had the great gift of allowing us to pour our love into him without any conditions. No one had to feel reservations about loving Dylan and Dylan had no reservations about loving us.

Dondi Tomkinson
Ashby, Massachusetts
October, 1997

Chapter One
INTRODUCTION

I used to visit sick and forgotten people in hospitals and nursing homes on holidays. I would often sit with them and listen, sometimes for hours, to their stories about where and how they grew up, their memories of bygone times, and the wonderful holidays, especially the Christmases, they used to spend with their families and friends who "are all gone now." Did I do any good by easing their pain a little? Maybe. That's something I'll never know. But there is something I have come to know for certain — that my dog, Dylan, had reached out farther, touched deeper and helped more people in his brief time on Earth than many humans, myself included, ever will.

This story in words and mostly pictures is about Dylan's life and work (and play, too) and his ability to truly connect with people to accomplish in five minutes more than most could accomplish in five hours.

Dylan at Two Years Old

Dylan's Story

Dylan was a Golden Retriever, a breed of dog that is known for its intelligence, sensitivity and good natured gentleness. Goldens are medium large dogs with thick floppy ears, expressive brown eyes, long wavy golden fur and a ready smile for strangers and friends alike. I see this breed as a paradox in the dog world. They are smart enough to guide the blind, yet dumb enough to take a nap in the middle of the street. Dylan had all the classic characteristics of his breed.

I don't happen to believe dogs (and other animals) are akin to obedient objects or to be used for any purpose. Dylan, as well as all of my other pets who preceded him, assured me and many others that animals of all kinds (even humans) have a unique spirit of life in them that sets them apart. I can say with certainty that I never met an animal of any kind that I considered an object. What's more, I am strongly against slavery so I would not give orders or consider myself their "master" or "owner." Consequently (despite my having to compromise in obedience classes), my pets tended to happily respond to my requests and were able to be their "own" selves.

Often people believe dogs are more like objects to obey commands and do what they're told, or to occupy the kids, or to be "fur babies" for would be, or wistful, mothers and fathers. . .or to bring distinction and prestige to those who tend to need it by winning championships, or to work the fields, or to retrieve ducks and other wildlife their people just killed. I find nothing wrong with feeling these ways. It's just that my perspective happens to be slightly different.

Occasionally, if one is lucky, an animal might come into one's life who has a special talent beyond his or her unique personality. Dylan was such a being. Having perceived this, I considered it my responsibility to do whatever was necessary to see that he could fulfill his mission in life. In his case, I realized that I would need to see that he had a life that would present to him opportunities to do what I believed he was meant to do — help people.

With that goal in mind, I chose to teach this puppy to become a certified therapy dog. This allowed him into places where there were people who needed his help. In the early 1990s, not as many people were familiar with therapy dogs as there are today. I hadn't given it much thought back then until I had the need to research the subject, having found myself with a Golden puppy who clearly had a talent to establish authentic relationships with people. Since I was unwilling to give him up to be a Seeing Eye dog, or a Hearing Ear dog, or any kind of Special Needs dog, it was up to me to teach both of us about applied pet therapy.

This was not a direction I had intended to go, but because I found myself with a dog who seemed to share a life purpose similar to my own — which was to be of service to others in whatever way was required, we started out on this journey together.

Therapy dogs are no longer as new on the social medicine scene as they were then, although the therapeutic relationship between humans and animals is as old as historians and anthropologists can trace. Prehistoric humans left clues that they were helped by animals. They domesticated cats, dogs, and horses. Probably the earlier applications of domesticated animals were more as aides in hunting for food and as beasts of burden for carrying heavy loads for people.

The old and very strong bonds haven't changed, so it is no surprise that animals continue to be wonderful helpmates. The evolution of changes was not in the relationship between animals and humans, but rather in the nature and variety of human needs. For example, instead of hauling or hunting (excluding those engaged in sports), the needs people have are less physical. Nowadays, pets serve people's emotional wellbeing and physical limitations. Above all else, I observed the most common, universal need people have is for someone to genuinely care about them.

The idea of animal-facilitated social, emotional, occupational, and physical therapies emerged after the development of the psychological sciences. The use of animals to support human functioning is especially important in long-term care and for those with physical disabilities. Studies have shown that people become happier, more communicative, and saner when given an animal to open up to and confide in. Pets may have kept many out of mental institutions. Dylan and I found depression in abundance, especially in long-term care facilities. That was the reason I made sure that Dylan wore silly costumes on holiday visits. No matter how depressed and discouraged one may feel, who could possibly resist smiling or even laughing when they saw a silly Halloween pumpkin with a serious look on his face enter their hospital room to see them?

"Yes, I'm right here. We all are."

A good example of depression healing is that of the relationship that developed between Larry and Dylan. It was due to Dylan's unrestricted love that Larry was able to trust Dylan's faithfulness and work through some deep and prolonged grief. Whenever Dylan drew near him, Larry would start to cry and call Dylan the names of every dog he used to have and had lost over his lifetime. All Dylan needed to do was to stand in for each and every one of those beloved pets to help Larry through his sorrow.

Pets relieve anxieties and act as emotional stabilizers because of the way they unconditionally accept us. I can't help thinking how enriched our lives would be if we humans took notice of this practice and included it more into our relationships with others.

Pets are not a panacea to all ills, but they clearly are an integral component of many types of healing. Dylan surely was.

I asked if TDI would kindly remove the word "owner" from Dylan's ID card, but as you can see, I was unsuccessful.

Chapter Two
A LITTLE HISTORY

Unlike the rest of us, Dylan started out as a puppy. He was born in a small town called Ashburnham in Massachusetts on February 20, 1993. His mom, Lady Brandy Alexandra XXXIII (Brandy), and his dad, Golden Jester II, (Boomer), had nine little golden puppies - five boys and four girls.

Dylan was in the middle of his litter in both birth order and size. However, he was not like most new puppies who are unable to focus for longer than a second. When I picked him up for the first time, he just looked at me without any of the typical hyperactivity of such a young animal.

Even as early as eight weeks old, Dylan showed signs of having the makings of a service dog. He could look directly at me and maintain eye contact longer than any puppy I had ever met. However, if Dylan became a service dog, it would mean that I would have to relinquish him to his calling. This thought triggered my research into therapy dog services so giving him away wouldn't be necessary. From then on I was determined that he learned to become an accomplished therapy dog.

Throughout his puppyhood, Dylan exhibited attentiveness to whatever he was learning about life. As part of his development I asked him to learn many things in addition to the usual dog stuff that

"I guess she's my family now."

most puppies are not required to learn. For example, I asked him to continually make longer and longer contact with others, identify people in the household, and follow the direction of my finger when I pointed to something. All of his stuffed toys had different names in anticipation of teaching him to differentiate various people by name. I made sure to hold him safely and comfortably on his back for long periods to continue to build his trust.

Along with this continual sensitivity training we attended puppy kindergarten which culminated in a group howl at graduation. Naturally, we went through all levels of obedience classes after that. Despite the fact that I don't like to use the 'obedience' word, being against slavery of all kinds, Dylan wasn't bothered by it and enjoyed the company of other puppies almost as much as he enjoyed doing the work. However, he was not just a dog's dog. He was an equal opportunity species lover.

Puppyhood

Even though Dylan was on a serious learning path to become of service to others, I made sure that there was balance in his life with lots of play time.

"How did she get it to bounce?"

From the very beginning he discovered that life was all about relationships (and food). Learning about many different relationships was the foundation of his preparation to become an effective instrument of healing.

When Dylan came to his new home, he discovered his family had another member in it besides me — an older feline friend and brother named Theodore.

Theod (for short) was extremely happy to have a new puppy finally, after five years of being an only pet since his beloved Chocolate Lab, Hershey, died. These two guys happened to be the same color and even the same size for one entire month.

Dylan and his older brother, Theod

As with most older brothers, it was Theod's responsibility to show his puppy the ropes. This included where the best spots to explore in the woods were, how to get what you wanted from humans, when it paid to be cute, and even how to survive visits to the vet. Dylan discovered that Theod knew everything there was to know about the world and was glad to teach him things. To broaden one's range of knowledge it was as important to deepen it, like digging holes in the back yard.

Theod showing his puppy where and how to walk in the woods.

Playing with children was important to learn about too because sometimes, as much as they may like you, they could hug you one minute and pull on your ears and step on you in the next moment. That usually didn't happen, but when it did, Dylan was not surprised and took it as a matter of course. What did happen most of the time is that children continuously asked Dylan to do things that had nothing to do with being a dog.

For his first four years, Dylan lived in a huge house with his main person, Linda (coincidentally the author of this book), and other people who rented space in her house. This was an excellent environment in which to raise a budding therapy dog. There were always

Rich is reading the nightly bedtime story to Alison, Jennifer, and Puppy Dylan

9

several kinds of humans around including children and grownups for a puppy to learn their ways. One of the many benefits of being raised in that household was being read captivating bedtime stories.

After story time, it was off to bed with Duckie (who was really a platypus).

"What are pedals?"

"Oh no. Cruella is going to steal those spotted puppies."

One day, Rich came inside and announced that there were little ducklings in the back yard. When Dylan heard the word "ducklings",

he misunderstood and thought Rich was asking him to get Duckie, which he did. When he went outside and saw what Rich was talking about, he had a sudden case of Duckie Confusion.

"These are Duckies? But I have Duckie in my mouth."

11

When the ducklings noticed Dylan, they assumed their mother had arrived. They followed him around the yard until Dylan came to the back door looking for assistance.

"I'm not really their mother, am I?"

Chapter Three
LIFEWORK

Building on a groundwork of kindness and connections, being of service to others is a rather broad goal that called for more specificity in actual endeavors.

Therapeutic Work

Dylan started working at health care facilities when he was only 5 months old. I didn't intend for him to start working so young. Initially I just wanted him to get accustomed to the peculiar smells of a hospital and a nursing home. I also wanted him to get the feel for slippery floor tiles and to become familiar with the noises, smells, and appliances used in these places, especially canes, crutches, wheel chairs, and walkers.

We were invited to The Highlands in Fitchburg to initiate him into the health care facility environment and start his training. I put a short curb leash on him until I could be sure that he wouldn't knock anyone down by mistake. Within 30 minutes I knew without a doubt that I could remove it after seeing how careful he was. He proved to be a natural and the Highlands medical director "hired" him on the spot. So much for easing Dylan into things.

Aside from his on-the-job training period in Fitchburg, the first person we went to visit was Guy, an Ashby resident who was in the Quabbin Valley Health Care facility in Orange, Massachusetts. It was after witnessing that visit that Quabbin Valley Health Care "hired"

Dylan to cover all of their patients. At this point, I had to set up a separate calendar for Dylan. Mine was already full.

Dylan's first visit to Quabbin Valley was to see Guy from Ashby.

Flexibility is an essential skill for a sensitive therapy dog because everybody wants you to do different things. If I wasn't in the area sending Dylan direction, he got so that he could figure out what to do if the person's need wasn't obvious. He learned how to "make the dog available" if the person's desired approach was unclear. That meant that he would stand or sit a little distance from the individual and wait for their response. The answer would become clear in short order. If the person shied away or said the word "allergic" or "I don't like dogs" he would immediately leave the room, unoffended. If a hand was extended, he would move close enough to allow himself to be petted. If both arms opened, he moved in to snuggle.

Holding hands with Doris

Dylan's progress far exceeded my expectations based on his early indoctrination and training. However, it turned out to be a mutual learning process when he and the residents of the health care facilities taught me a thing or two along the way. One thing I learned was that his talent was so natural I could trust him very quickly to do no harm. I also discovered after just two visits that this was not merely training. He had started his work.

This was our therapeutic paradigm and how it worked: when Dylan and I entered a hospital room or a room with a group of people, I would rapidly assess the situation, including who was there, what their needs were and which needs were more immediate. This was very similar to the triage process in emergency rooms except our process was not based on critical physical conditions, but rather psychological and emotional conditions. Once I had gauged the situation, I gave Dylan a silent signal to direct him to the most urgent area requiring his focus. All the while, Dylan had been watching me for that signal. As soon as he received it, he approached the targeted individual and sensitively engaged in a relationship with that person. Once that happened, I would step away and take over the vigilant watcher role from a distance so that I could perform any adjustments that may have been needed.

"Fran is waiting for her turn to touch me. It won't be long now."

This way of working seemed to be quite different from the typical, albeit useful, model of the person's using the therapy dog as a way of making the connection between the patient and the person who brought the animal. As I mentioned, his work took various forms, all depending on the needs of the individuals he was serving in the moment. As it happened, when he went for his certification tests, I was told by the tough and exacting judge that I had overtrained him. It was not my intention to have him over-perform, but Dylan took it all in stride and our way with people seemed to touch them deeply.

The nature and benefits of our practice became obvious immediately. Facilitating and building relationships between Dylan and whoever he was with, leaving me out of it, was very powerful. This was unlike other working therapy dogs, even today, in which their person takes them to "visit" people while they strike up a conversation with the patient. I observed that, in many cases, the stress of expecting some patients to hold up their end of conversations detracted from the power and positive effects of the person-to-animal bond. With practice, Dylan learned to read

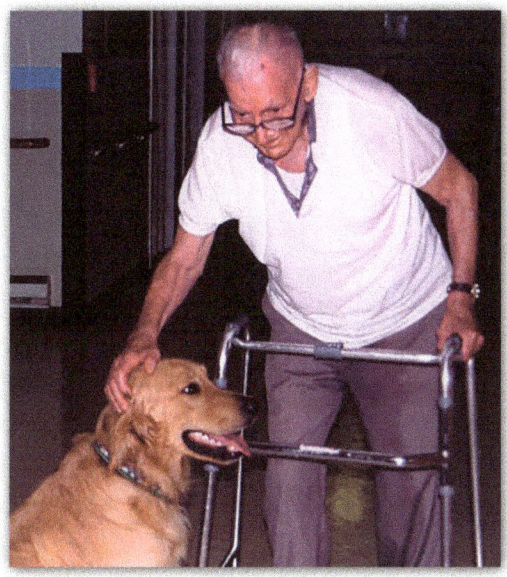

It's nice to have a dog to pet on your walk.

people he was serving and adapt to their immediate emotional needs thus eliminating the distraction for them to pay attention to me.

Sometimes it looked like Dylan felt embarrassed (if that's something dogs can feel) when numerous people told him how wonderful he was for devoting himself to so many people.

As a matter of fact, institutions and nonprofit organizations offered to pay for his services several times.

We, I mean, I, politely declined. At least I hope I was polite. They didn't have enough money to buy what Dylan was offering their patients, anyway.

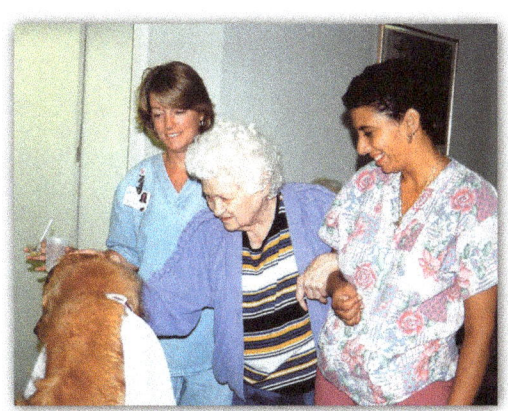

"He's pretty cute, isn't he Jean?"

This kind of treatment became Dylan's life on almost all Saturdays, Sundays and holidays. His schedule was challenging, but his work was a breeze.

As can be seen here with Marion, it appeared that Dylan enjoyed his work. It had to be done, somebody had to do it, and he was just the dog for the job.

Hugs are the Best

"I don't know why they call this work."

What may have looked like a wink was sometimes Dylan starting to fall asleep as he was being fussed over and cuddled. I'm somewhat sure he wasn't gloating. . .

18

"So, Dylan, I used to play ball, too."

"But, Stan, I never really liked playing ball. Rich would throw it and ask me to retrieve it. 'Here you go, Rich.' And then, you won't believe this — he threw it again one more time! I just stood there and looked at him. I wasn't about to fall for that trick again when clearly he didn't want the ball."

Although Dylan spent most of his work life in geriatrics, he didn't limit his services to merely one segment of society. He really didn't care how old you were or what you were "in" for.

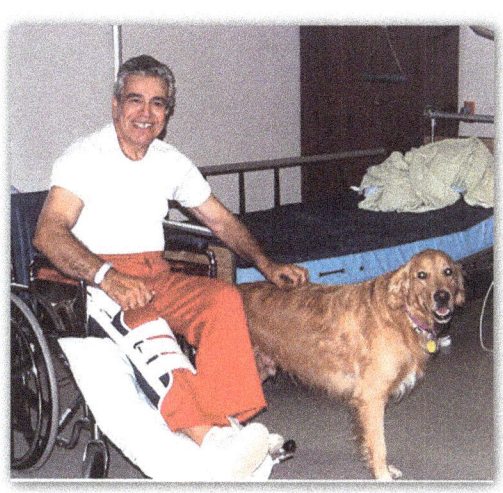

John was a short term guest in the hospital. He didn't need too much

As I mentioned previously, Dylan wasn't the only one in the learning process. His typical practice to make contact was to sit in a chair next to the bed of someone confined and offer his paw for holding or his head for petting. Whatever way the person needed in order to touch him. But Helen had to have the safety guard rail up for her protection and she couldn't get as close to Dylan as she wanted. This caused her to ask me if Dylan could get in bed with her. I said that it was not a good idea in case he might accidentally roll on her hip or other fragile bones. Helen insisted that he would not do that. I looked at Dylan who was giving me the same look that Helen was. I appreciated that he was sure he would be careful not to cause any harm. After some hesitation, I told them that we would carefully try it and that I would stay nearby instead of leaving the room as was my usual practice.

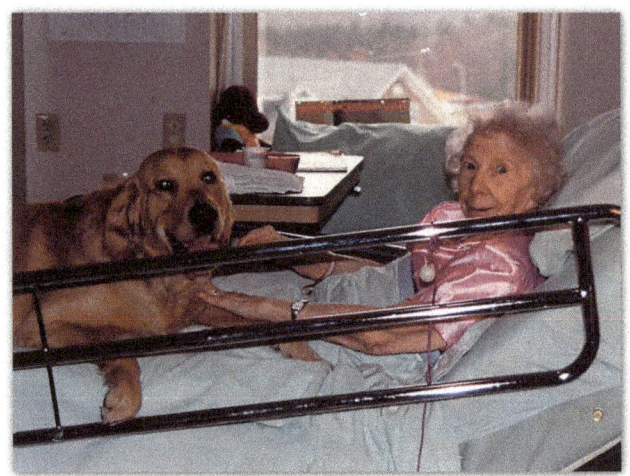

Dylan in bed with Helen

After watching them for a while, I saw that I could trust both of them to be very careful and I left the room. I learned my lesson. As the word got around among nurses and patients, this arrangement caught on and Dylan was requested to join others in their beds after that.

Another popular way that patients enjoyed connecting with Dylan when they were confined to bed, was having him at their level. They were amused seeing him in a wheelchair with a "johnny" on until they got used to seeing him being one of them and just accepted and loved it.

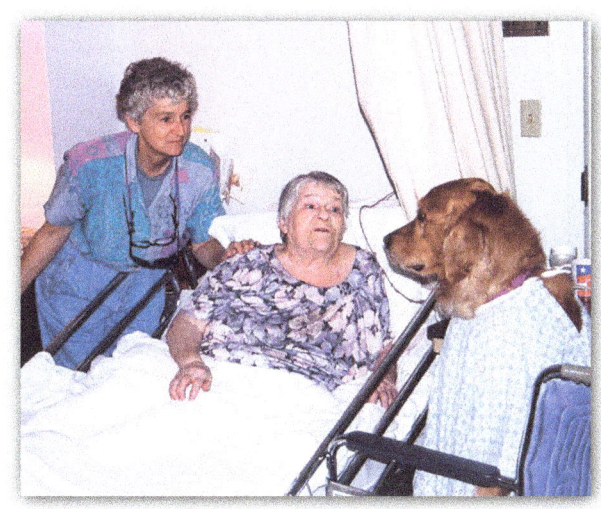

"Did you hear what they're serving us for lunch today?"

In Group watching a movie with the guys.

He would sit in a regular chair without a hospital gown in group settings to join the people in their activities. Although he tried, Dylan wasn't too successful participating if the group objective was exercise. However, he did try to participate when everyone was asked to move just their arms and not their legs.

Humans usually don't inspire this beautiful glow on the faces of others. Hopefully, we will all want to learn how to do that someday without having to be cute with fur.

"Evelyn really loves me."

"My name is Dillon, too, but it isn't spelled like yours. Since you probably don't read it doesn't matter. We have the same name."

Father Dillon was a retired Roman Catholic priest. As they came to know each other they discovered that both Dillon and Dylan were committed to serving people. The two Ds formed a very strong bond that didn't rely on their sharing names.

D y l a n was asked to do many d i f f e r e n t things. In this case he was faced with a dilemma because he knew he was not allowed to kiss people on the face.

"Are you sure you want me to kiss your face, Mary?"

"This is more like it."

Fortunately, the hesitation was understood and resolved.

A lot of flexibility is required when you are a dog being asked to be in places and to do things that requires you to understand and satisfy requests. Despite this challenge, it never took Dylan very long to get the idea and respond accordingly. The understanding part required more than intuition and subtle clues. A substantial vocabulary was also needed — such as knowing that your paw is also considered your hand.

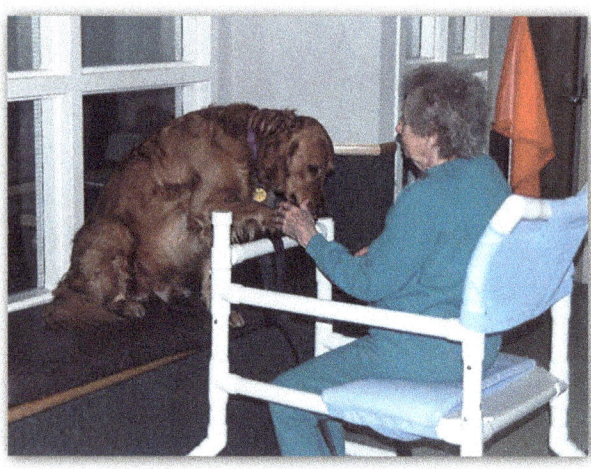

"You want me up on this ledge, Helen? And then you want my hand? Okay."

I was a little surprised when patients wanted Dylan to accompany them to their physical therapy sessions. I understood how painful it was to move when it hurt a lot, but I never considered how having a dog in the area watching helped. He clearly couldn't cheer them on. I guess being able to look at him from time to time, seeing that he was watching you closely felt like he was cheering you on. That's just a guess.

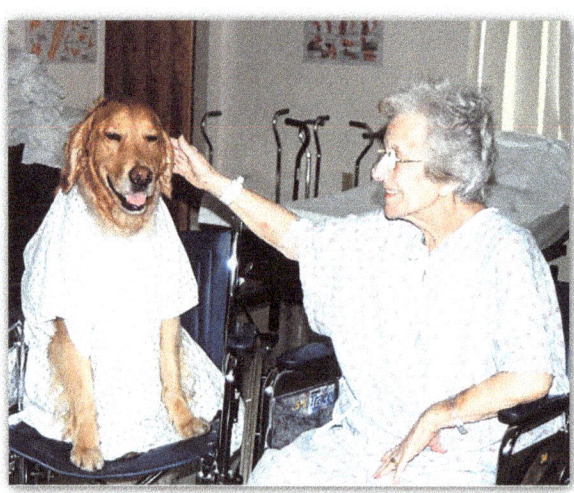

"Thanks for coming to Physical Therapy with me, Dylan. I usually don't enjoy it so"

At one point, staff from the Occupational Therapy department spoke to me about a challenge that they had with one of their

patients. Marilyn was an extremely intelligent PhD who taught at MIT for years before she suffered a serious stroke, leaving her left arm paralyzed for several months. The staff tried everything they could to encourage her to try to regain use of her arm by squeezing balls and stretching it in various ways. She had such a hard time with it that she just wouldn't do any of the exercises she was given.

Occupational Therapy borrowed Dylan to entice Marilyn to move her arm.

Two of the OT therapists wondered if there was any way Dylan might be helpful because they had observed Marilyn on several occasions looking lovingly at him. She didn't smile about too many things, but she did whenever she saw Dylan. So they took Dylan over to her and sat him down a short distance from her, but not too close, and asked her to touch him, feel his soft fur, and give him some love pats. That day we all cheered as Marilyn struggled, but succeeded to move her arm to reach him. Needless to say, Dylan spent time with Marilyn from then on as she regained the use of her left arm.

I'm not sure how this made me an expert, but I accepted invitations from Becker University to lecture their Occupational Therapy classes. Dylan accompanied me to demonstrate, of course.

Sometimes we sat with friends we had known for years. Kay performed in many of my shows as well as being the lead soprano in her own church choir. Dylan relaxed so much I think I'd consider his visits with Kay as strictly social.

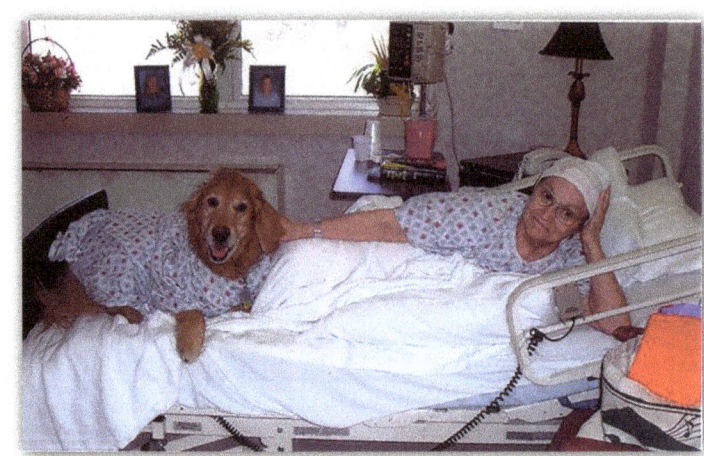

Dylan with our friend, Kay

"We dogs are not totally color blind. That goes on a red nine. I do have trouble seeing red though."

"They gave us turkey for lunch. Then my son came to visit and we watched some TV together."

"...and that's how my day went..."

Some people, especially on the Alzheimer's floor, would reverse the traditional practice of dogs drooling on people. There were people in those areas that could be counted on to drool on the dog.

They couldn't help it and there was always an orderly or nurse immediately on the spot to clean up any drool on Dylan. Apologies tended to follow, but it was okay. We knew what we had signed up for. Merely seeing  some of these people connect with the "here and now" because of Dylan was gratifying.

There were some people afflicted with Alzheimer's who loved pushing Dylan up and down the hallways in a wheelchair. Invariably they would come back to the group room without him. The attendants and I knew when this happened that we would have to go look for Dylan. After searching the halls and rooms we would eventually find him still in his wheelchair in some corner, patiently waiting until someone came for him.

"So, Mary, did you notice there are no dog biscuits in here?"

"Now let's see if we can figure out what's wrong."

*"Good news. You're not sick, just exhausted from getting
so much kissing, hugging, and cuddling."*

Holidays and Ceremonies

Holidays are emotional times for most and especially for those who Dylan took care of. The happy memories of celebrating holidays from their long gone past was difficult to bear. Hospitals and health

care facilities decorated the halls and provide special holiday meals, but this didn't quite touch the emotional nature of their longings. That need was met when family members and friends came to visit, if there were any left and who were near enough to do so. We made sure their melancholy was addressed when Dylan provided that missing link as well as or better than any non-relative could.

The Christmas Reindeer

It was also very important to many that we not to overlook the religious

The Nativity Sheep

The Pilgrim

Granting that Christmas tended to be the holiday that brought back remembrances of the biggest loss for many people, it seemed that Thanksgiving was a close second. After many years of one's life spent with their family and friends, cooking together, enjoying the wonderful aromas from the kitchen, watching traditional movies and sports on television after the delicious meal, and perhaps playing games in the evening while snacking on leftovers, it was understandable that the disappearance of one's friends and family members hurt a great deal. Even though spending time with a canine pilgrim was no total antidote for holiday melancholy, it was difficult for most patients to grieve and hurt so badly when presented with someone who was so serious while appearing quite silly.

The whimsical fun of Halloween wasn't as poignant as Christmas and Thanksgiving reminiscences, but nevertheless, important to remind people how necessary it is to enjoy the lighter things in life.

Marion with the Great Pumpkin

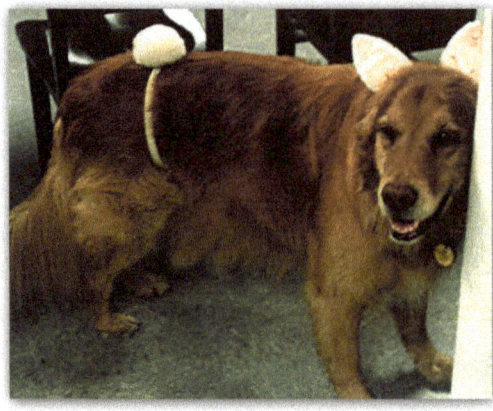

The Easter Bunny? You get the idea...

There were many Christian people whose most important religious holiday was Easter. Although the Easter Bunny was not exactly their connection with the doctrine, it was at least a reminder of the childhood meaning of the holiday.

In addition to acknowledging holidays, there was one critical observance that occurred periodically when working with very ill people and many elderly folks. The first time Dylan's presence was requested at a funeral service was on a Saturday when we entered Bill's hospital room to find his wife, Lucille, by his bedside. Bill had passed away just moments before we arrived. I expressed my condolences and suggested we leave her to be with him when she said, "No, please come in. Bill loved Dylan so much. Would it be okay if Dylan sat with me next to Bill for a while?" I said, "Of course," and asked Dylan to get in the chair next to the bed. Lucille had her hand on Bill's arm while Dylan snuggled in with his muzzle on both Bill's arm and Lucille's hand.

The Flowers Dylan Brought

32

After some time had passed and the two of them moved from the bedside, Lucille asked me if Dylan could come to Bill's funeral. I was a bit surprised because I had never thought about this before. I told Lucille that if she spoke with her clergy about her request and they agreed, that we would attend. I gave her my phone number and she called the next day and told me that her minister thought it was an important request and that he would be honored to have Dylan there.

On our way to the service, we stopped at a florist and I bought a small bouquet of white carnations for Dylan to take to the service. As we drove into the parking lot, I was preparing to explain to the attendants why I had a dog with me, but as they opened my door for me they said, "This must be master Dylan." All I needed to say was "yes" because they were expecting him. So much for my trying to figure out how to explain the situation.

By the time I signed the register and walked into the service area, Dylan had gone ahead and was already shaking hands with family members in the receiving line. He had carefully placed his bouquet in front of Lucille. I could hear the "ahhh"s from the already

seated congregation. After acknowledging Lucille and meeting the rest of Bill's family, I took Dylan and his flowers over to the casket and asked him to lie down with the bouquet in front of him and post sentry. That's where he stayed for the entire service while I joined the congregation. When it was time to close the casket, Lucille went over to Dylan and, with Dylan now beside her, she placed Dylan's flowers in the casket. Then she and Dylan stood together while she said her "goodbyes." I heard a lot of crying around me. It was such a touching scene that it opened up people to their own grief. As we were leaving, I was asked by the minister if I would consider loaning Dylan out to do other funerals. I smiled at him as we left.

The word spread like wild fire, generating requests from others. When invited, I did take him to other funeral and memorial services, but only for his friends.

Every year we were invited to dine with staff and other volunteers of healthcare facilities in the area. These events were not my favorite things to do, but Dylan loved them. He managed to be the center of attention, which suited him, but as a well-practiced recluse when I wasn't working, they were a bit too social for me.

Attending an Evening Awards Banquet for Volunteers

Public Service

Until 1997, when Dylan was four years old, I was still working as a senior group engineering manager for Digital Equipment Corporation — work that frequently took me away from our home in Ashby. In July of that year I received a call from the Town of Ashby's Selectmen's office to ask me to help in Ashby's town government while they looked for a

"I didn't know there were so many dog laws."

35

new Town Administrator. After fourteen years of having to be away a lot, the three-minute commute they were offering sounded quite appealing. I agreed to work as the "interim" Town Administrator to help out while encouraging them to hire someone with a Master's degree in public administration (not comparative literature and psychology). As it happened, the "interim" designation eventually disappeared thirteen years later when I accepted a position in Rockport and Ashby finally hired a Town Administrator.

It was such a relief to be home more and much easier to keep up with Dylan's busy schedule as well as my own. I was able to take him to work with me every day, where he became a fixture and helper by carrying messages to the various Town Hall offices as requested (leaving minimal dog spit on them).

During one evening meeting of the Ashby Board of Selectmen, there was an ambulance call to which one of the Selectmen who was a paramedic responded, thus interrupting the Selectmen's annual appointment process. While the remaining board

"If I only had fingers…"

members were discussing other town business before resuming making the rest of the appointments, they received a call from Eleanor, a resident who was watching the meeting on television. She told them that her aunt was visiting from Connecticut and wanted to meet the "Town Hall Dog." After they invited Eleanor to bring her aunt to the meeting they turned around and woke up Dylan who was in his usual meeting spot behind them, napping after putting in a full day's work. At that point, on a lark, one of them made a motion to appoint Dylan as "Town Hall Dog." The Board immediately voted in the affirmative.

What began as a lighthearted gesture to endorse the resident's sobriquet turned into an unexpected publicity action. The next day the Town Clerk received a call from a reporter asking when she would be swearing the Town Hall Dog into office. After checking her calendar, she said she would do that on Wednesday.

Top dog, officially

The Associated Press

Town Clerk Dianne M. Enus administers the oath of office Wednesday to the official Town Hall Dog, Dylan, a golden retriever, in Ashby, Mass. A certified therapy dog belonging to Town Administrator Linda Sanders, Dylan donned a tie and obediently raised his paw after the Ashby Board of Selectmen gave him the distinction.

"Portland Press Herald" on Friday July 14, 2000

Newspapers across the country picked up the story from the Associated Press. My assistant forwarded a call to me from the "Tonight Show", asking if Dylan could come on the show and do some tricks. I politely declined and explained that Dylan was already famous enough for his therapeutic services. I limited his acting to community theater.

Board appoints town hall dog to position

ASHBY, Mass.

No dog days of summer for Dylan.

The 7-year-old golden retriever, already a well-known furry face around town, is the new town hall dog.

Last week, the Board of Selectmen officially appointed him to the position for the fiscal year 2001. It's a position he's held unofficially since 1997, when his owner, town administrator Linda Sanders, began her job.

Perks include a listing in the phone book under the town clerk's office staff.

Dylan has also worked with geriatrics as a therapy dog, helped out the Red Cross disaster services team, and even acted in community theater, starring as Sandy in a production of "Annie."/AP

"The Napa Valley Register"
on July 7, 2000

Needless to say, Dylan became somewhat of a celebrity while I crossed my fingers that all the publicity wouldn't make Ashby look silly. Fortunately, it turned out to be quite the contrary. It was much more dignified to be considered charming rather than ridiculous.

Community Service

Dylan was asked to march in Memorial Day parades with the Friends of Ashby, a non-profit volunteer organization that helped local people in need. They readily accepted him as a member. Fortunately, he was not required to attend their meetings.

He never seemed to tire of participating in community events. As a matter of fact, he participated in Ashby's First Parish Church's

"Don't worry. I won't drop the flag."

annual Blessing of the Animals ceremony held on Ashby Common every October.

While still working for the Town, Dylan also helped me with one of Ashby's major construction projects to expand the library. When

the project was successfully completed, the Board of Library Trustees asked him to join them in the Grand Opening of the new wing of the Ashby Library, whose construction he helped me manage.

"Need any more digging done?"

Dylan at the Library

Dylan and I received many invitations to visit people in their homes when they couldn't get around too well any more. These two were absolutely wonderful people whose home visit felt more like getting together with friends.

A home visit with Bob and Esther

They had a cat, but I don't think she was too fond of dogs because I had to get down on my hands and knees to meet her under a bed. Dylan was unused to having a cat be afraid of him, leaving him somewhat confused.

Another Community Service group Dylan was asked to join was the **American Red Cross Disaster Services Team**. They wanted him to be a Comfort Dog to help people who became immobile with shock and grief, such as those who lost their homes in fires or who had lost family members as a result of terrible disasters of any kind. On many sad occasions people benefitted from Dylan's tenderness.

"The Montachusett Telegram & Gazette" on May 28, 1997

So much to do, so little time. . .

t's a therapy dog's life

George W. Barnes II
Writer

LEOMINSTER — Dylan isn't a search dog. He won't find drugs or locate a bomb — but if you need a hug, he does good hugs.

The 4-year-old golden retriever from Ashby is a therapy dog, trained to heal by comforting. If you're feeling down he tends to sense it.

He normally works with elderly nursing home patients, but he and owner Linda Sanders met with members of the North Central Massachusetts Chapter of the American Red Cross Tuesday to talk about ways he could help out victims of fires and other disasters.

"We're exploring possible ways of affiliating him with our chapter," said Lori Tsagronis, director of emergency services for the local Red Cross chapter.

Tsagronis said it is likely the dog would not be used at the scene, but would help at shelters or in other places once the victims are away from the scene.

Sanders said Dylan has worked mostly with elderly people, regularly visiting the highlands Nursing Home in Fitchburg and Quabbin Valley Healthcare in Athol since he was five months old.

"For the past 3½ years, every Saturday we have been at one of these places," she

Sanders said Dylan has been invited to birthday parties of people he got to know at nursing homes and has been asked to take part in funerals.

If she can find the time, Sanders said she hopes to bring the dog to visit hospitalized children as well.

Dylan has been trained from puppyhood, and has achieved designations of "canine good citizen," and "companion dog." Sanders said his training is ongoing.

"We're always running into new situations," she said.

Tsagronis said therapy dogs were used in the wake of the Oklahoma City federal building bombing to help disaster workers deal with the stress of the rescue efforts.

In this area, she said Dylan's services to the Red Cross would be unique.

See THERAPY, Page A8

Sentinel & Enterprise / JULIA CHENG

Lori Tsagronis, Director of Emergency Services for the Leominster Red Cross gives a drink of water to Dylan, a golden retriever and certified therapy dog.

'He is dedicated to serving humanity, and we'll do everything we can do to help out.'

Linda Sanders
Dylan's owner

"Sentinel & Enterprise" on April 16, 1997

. . . and constantly in the news.

Our commitment to serve others was already heavily taxing our two schedules so, of course, we added another one. I agreed to participate in the annual **Bereavement Workshops for Children** sponsored by the **VNA Hospice** organization of Lowell, Massachusetts in conjunction with the Lowell General Hospital and their Visiting Nurses group. At that time, twenty-some years ago, younger children's grief tended to be overlooked and became subservient to the grownups' shock and heartbreak as older siblings and parents tearfully coped with their own losses. Fortunately, things have changed for the better over the years. Families have become much better at attending to their children's fears and sadness. But back then, these little kids were suffering and had no idea what to do about it. So they stubbornly buried their intense pain and were too frightened to let their feelings out.

These excellent organizations saw the critical need and facilitated the grieving process for children from the ages of 5 years old to 17 years old. We were assigned to lead the 5 to 7 year old group along with several counselors who were there for support if the children needed them.

There were always pre-session meetings wherein all of us were briefed on the particular situation of every child. The workshops began after a brief introductory talk in assembly before we went to our separate rooms. There were typically between 8 to 12 children in our youngest group. They were instructed to bring a picture of the person who died in their lives. Usually, it would be a family member, although once in a while it would be a young friend. They would hesitantly enter our room, where they found Dylan lying in the middle of the floor with a picture of his brother, Theod, beside him.

I would invite them to form a circle around Dylan and place their photos in front of them. The social workers and psychotherapists would take their places behind the children in case they were needed.

We used Dylan to reach the children because they were holding on so tightly to their trauma. I told them that I would speak to them for Dylan because he only spoke "dog," which is not easily understood by people. With the several therapists ready to catch any child who may have needed it, I pushed hard to break through the protective walls they had built. I told them that the picture of the yellow cat was Dylan's best friend and brother. I described how much Dylan loved to eat, sleep, and play with Theod. Then one day Theod didn't want to play or snuggle any more. It turned out that he was sick and had to go to the veterinary hospital for help. When he eventually came home, Theod seemed a little better. And then he died!

At first Dylan didn't understand where he went. He looked all through the house and outside, but couldn't find him. Finally it sank into him that he would never see Theod again. Dylan felt afraid and he was kind of mad that Theod left him all alone. And then Dylan's heart began to hurt so badly that he didn't know what to do. As you may imagine, I pushed these little kids so hard that they weren't able to hold on to their protective barriers.

I invited each one into the center of the circle with their picture and told them that Dylan really wanted to know who died in their family. Although intense, the process worked. For example, I will never forget the little 5 year old girl named Kelsey. She was determined to hold her armor and came into the circle reluctantly. She began to pet Dylan and then snuggled and lifted his ear to tell him who died in her family. She whispered in it and said "my mommy." There was a small boy named David who entered the circle with a photograph of his father who I learned at the briefing had killed himself. I asked him what he understood about how his daddy died and he shrugged his shoulders and told Dylan that is wasn't cancer. I said, "that's right, Dylan. It wasn't cancer, it was depression." Thereafter David had a way to talk to others about losing his father due to a disease. There are many such recollections I carry with me over the years since, about all those suffering children and how, by the end of the day, they would be outside playing with Dylan while the emotional freedom started seeping into their beings.

Rainbow Bridge

Just this side of heaven is a place called Rainbow Bridge.

When an animal dies that has been especially close to someone here, that pet goes to Rainbow Bridge.
There are meadows and hills for all of our special friends so they can run and play together.
There is plenty of food, water and sunshine, and our friends are warm and comfortable.

All the animals who had been ill and old are restored to health and vigor; those who were hurt or maimed are made whole and strong again, just as we remember them in our dreams of days and times gone by.
The animals are happy and content, except for one small thing; they each miss someone very special to them, who had to be left behind.

They all run and play together, but the day comes when one suddenly stops and looks into the distance. His bright eyes are intent; His eager body quivers. Suddenly he begins to run from the group, flying over the green grass, his legs carrying him faster and faster.

You have been spotted, and when you and your special friend finally meet, you cling together in joyous reunion, never to be parted again. The happy kisses rain upon your face; your hands again caress the beloved head, and you look once more into the trusting eyes of your pet, so long gone from your life but never absent from your heart.

Then you cross Rainbow Bridge together....

Author unknown...

In addition to the grief of losing friends and family members, the loss of family pets was also addressed, with Dylan there. I have no idea who wrote the "Rainbow Bridge," but it seemed to comfort the children. We used it every year.

Needless to say, Dylan and I were both exhausted when we arrived home after these sessions. I told myself that, yes, we could do it again for just one day every year.

Although not a recurring commitment like the others mentioned, we participated in an "After the Loss" workshop put on by the **American Cancer Society**. It was a weekend retreat called the "We Can Weekend!"

I'm not sure why they thanked me only when Dylan did most of the "front-end" work while I just unobtrusively directed him. I listened and encouraged the patients while he made the life-affirming contacts.

Retirement

It happens to all of us who make it to that "age" — retirement. It happened to Dylan after 10 years of loyally "being there" for countless people who needed so badly for someone to care **about** them. This practice should not be confused with having someone care **for** them. The dedicated medical professionals had that well-covered.

It didn't surprise me that so many individuals of all ages and backgrounds have no one in their lives who they know cares about them — or that many are unable to trust anyone to care about them as a result of prolonged periods of being mistreated by others. Whatever the reason, the cure is having reliable contact with someone who loves you and you definitely feel it and positively know it.

Dylan was the perfect medicine for this pervasive condition. He showed no signs of wanting to quit, but sadly, due to his own failing health, it became necessary. It had become increasingly harder for him to breathe. He had to retire because he couldn't keep being in places that needed to maintain such a high level of heat, especially in long-term living facilities. Consequently he retired on September 3, 2003.

The Highlands, where he began his career, threw him a big retirement party in their large function room. It looked like they invited everyone. As soon as we arrived, people greeted him at the door and took him right in to the

"Sentinel & Enterprise" on September 3, 2003

decorated room. I followed. There appeared to be over 200 people there. It never ceased to amaze me how popular Dylan was.

The majority in attendance included many of the friends he served over the years from several places, including the staffs of doctors, nurses, and attendants. Even public officials came to thank and honor him.

There was an abundance of refreshments, and gifts of toys and treats for Dylan. From his period of Public Service in Ashby, the chairman of the Board of Selectmen was there.

As if that wasn't impressive enough, the Mayor of Fitchburg and Massachusetts State Senator Brian Knuuttila attended. Senator Knuuttila presented Dylan with a Commendation and Certificate of

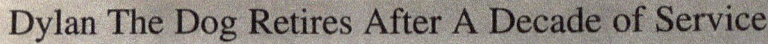

Dylan The Dog Retires After A Decade of Service

Fond Farewell to Ashby Dog

BY BETSY DILLBECK

ASHBY - It was raining last Friday afternoon, and the gentleman with the golden hair had an important date with a lot of folks who looked forward to his regular Saturday morning visits.

He was looking his best, his hair soft and silky, freshly groomed and brushed. If he knew it wasn't Saturday morning and that something was going on other than an ordinary visit, he never gave a clue. He donned his yellow hooded raincoat with the visor and headed for The Highlands, a nursing care facility behind Burbank Hospital. Once in the parking lot and out of the car, he knew exactly where to go.

At the main desk, he must have heard the clamor and activity coming from the main living room off of the lobby and headed right for it. As he entered, still in his slick yellow raincoat, and walked down the ramp, the "oohs" and "aahs" began, as people called his name and wanted to shake his hand – or rather, paw.

"He takes it for granted that people just love him,"

Dylan the Dog/Please turn to page 3

State Rep. Brian Knnuttila congratulates Dylan on his retirement from his Therapy Dog duties at The Highlands in Fitchburg. Also attending the retirement party was Ashby Selectman Michael McCallum. Behind Dylan is his owner, Ashby Town Administrator Linda Sanders.

Congratulations and Gratitude for his ten years of service to the senior citizens of North Central Massachusetts on behalf of the Speaker of the House of Representatives, Thomas Finneran.

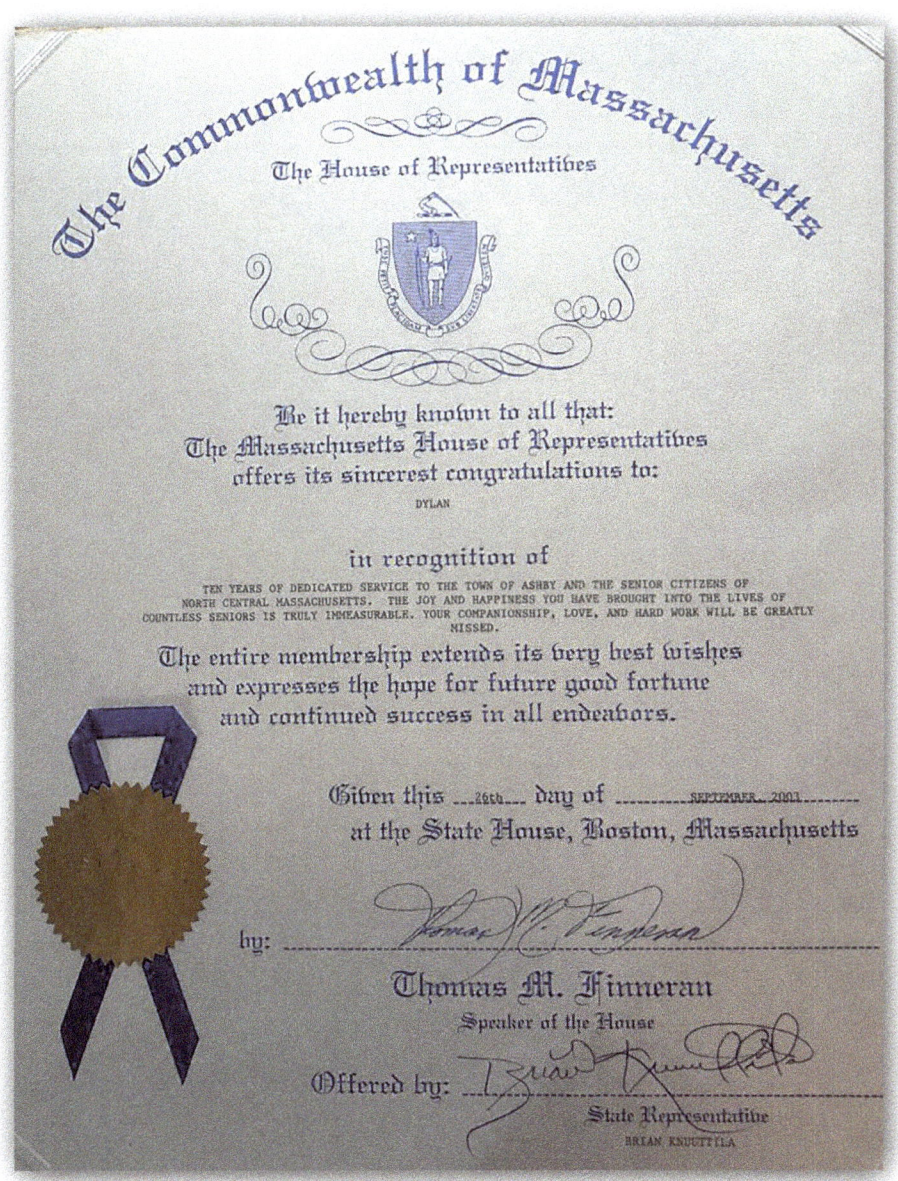

"The Community Journal" on October 3, 2003

How cool was that? Everyone was totally impressed except Dylan who took it all in with gratitude. Perhaps gratitude was what I was feeling. He just looked happy.

Chapter Four
OFF DUTY

Some dogs have sporting hobbies such as "frisbee" and "fetch the tennis ball" until the human thrower can't stand it anymore. Dylan (and I, especially), had been unable to cultivate a desire to participate in these sports. Instead we travelled, played with friends, and participated in community theater, mainly. It was not like we had much time to do any of these things, but over time, we managed to do some "off duty" things.

Travel and Sight Seeing

Dylan's first plane ride was from Boston to Phoenix to visit old friends of mine. Liz and Dave and their two boys had invited us for Thanksgiving one year. Since they liked to cook, it seemed to me like a good time to go.

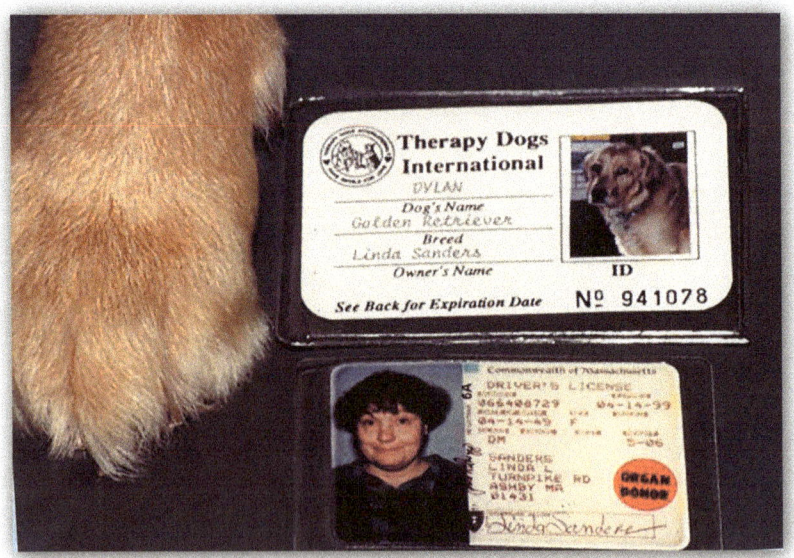

Our Travel IDs

I was accustomed to waiting around in airports because my high tech job often required me to travel to Europe where I had engineering, computer system designers and product management staff.

She was ready for a nap and found a soft place to rest.

I discovered that it was quite a different matter traveling with Dylan. For one thing, waiting to board was never boring. Just about eveyone waiting between planes wanted time with Dylan.

What I appreciated most, however, was how he managed to frequently get us bumped up to first class at the boarding gates. The flight attendants wanted to make sure that Dylan had more room and finer meals. I never minded going along for the ride.

How cute is this kid?

It looks like Dylan told her something funny.

There was one flight when we were returning on a Denver to Boston flight on which there were no available seats in first class, so I remained in my assigned economy seat. But of course, Dylan rode home in first class being fed well and pampered by attendants and first class passengers.

Sure it's okay to pet me as much as you like. I can take it.

One July, Dylan and I took the ferry to Nantucket for the day. Of course he turned out to be a hit on the crowded vessel. It was not only the passengers that fawned over him, but the Captain kept bringing him hot dog pieces from the food concession on board until I had to stop him. Dylan would have continued politely accepting the food beyond his capacity to ingest it.

On the Ferry to Martha's Vineyard

On the way to the island we were treated to seeing a whale very near the boat. I was amused

when I noticed that a nice stranger took over Dylan's first whale watching experience. It was amusing to the passengers and to me to watch the whale and to watch the unknown woman and Dylan watching the whale together.

I wasn't close enough to hear what she was telling him, but it was obvious that he was watching and listening intently.

Whale Watching

Another excursion we made was to North Carolina to experience a bit of good weather on the beach. . .

"I'm not sure what a sand castle is, but I can dig in the sand if you want."

and to play with kids. . .

In North Carolina with his friends, Jane and Jack

and to swim with friends Dylan had come to visit.

Hanging with Friends

Dylan had several close canine friends. Horton was one who lived in Athol, Massachusetts and was known around town as quite a character.

Good buddies, Dylan and Horton

One summer, Dylan's friend, Como was staying with us while her person was away. Como joined Dylan and me on a trip to Maine to visit their friend, Bonnie, who lived there with her person.

On vacation in Maine with his friends, Como and Bonnie, on their way to the beach.

As I recall, we had to wait for Dylan to get in the car because there was a fly on the seat he didn't want to hurt. So we all waited for the fly to leave.

55

While in Phoenix, Dylan accompanied his good friend Brian to his Cub Scout meeting...

"What does 'prepared' mean?"

and then joined Brian for a nap when they got home.

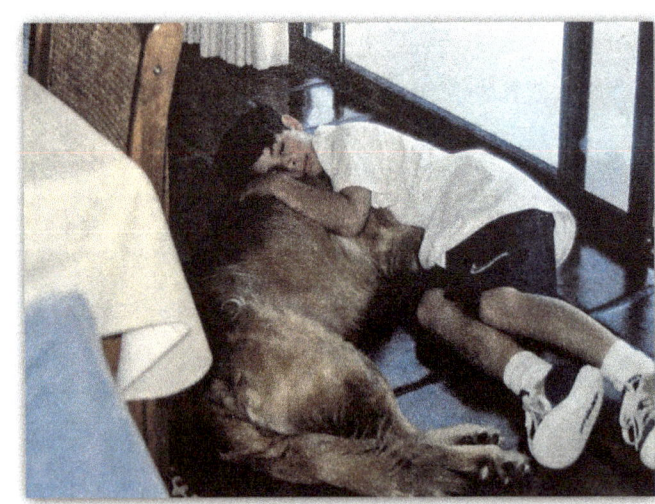

Nap time in Phoenix with Brian

Community Theater

As pastimes go, theater is not really feasible to fit into two busy schedules, but it happened to be my favorite hobby, so naturally, it became Dylan's whether he liked it or not. He liked it.

I remember hearing whispers from some people in the audience the first time the curtain opened and people saw Dylan on stage. "There's a dog on stage with no leash." It was overhearing those comments that reminded me of the short curb leash Dylan wore when he went to the Highlands to train on his first day of work. He wasn't even a year old and that was probably the last time he wore any kind of leash, including walking around the city of Boston on errands with me.

Anyway, Dylan was easy to direct on stage with hand signals. Since he was used almost as a prop and had no lines or musical numbers, he was one of the easiest actors to deal with.

I directed five shows over the years, two of which were musical revues. I was always busy behind, or in front of, the stage. Dylan was usually on it. The two musical revues were "Broadway Nights" for which I invited some gifted friends to Ashby from Broadway to complement the very good local talent.

People took many rehearsal photos. This one is from a production of "Annie". Dylan also played Snoopy from "You're a Good Dog, Charlie Brown," sitting on a doghouse in one of the revues. The audience couldn't tell

"Sandy" and "Annie" in rehearsal

there was a Golden inside the white tee shirt with black spots painted on it and two black and white Beagle ears that hung from the white head top. Actually, they could, and they were delighted.

In one of the shows, Dylan "performed" a jazz number behind a dormant mic with a picture of his idol, Lassie, on a table beside him. Meanwhile, Phil, a very talented jazz singer ghost sang for Dylan from the pit. For this performance Dylan received a standing ovation. The audience never noticed Phil who did all the work.

Dylan Singing the "Dog Bone Blues" in a Musical Revue

The most recent show I did was an original musical comedy. Dylan was long gone and, although I wrote a dog into the script, I didn't cast my current guy. Sky is very sweet, but he's more of a player than an actor.

Sky

Instead, I chose another talented canine to carry on the theatrical tradition. She was a beautiful girl in several scenes with various cast members who adored her.

CHARICLO MALCOLMSON *(Kitty) Living the Island Life* is Chariclo's theatrical debut. She was born in New Brunswick, Canada, and as a young pup joined her handler Elizabeth and the rest of the Malcolmson family in Rockport where she enjoys dog sports like agility and cart pulling. The Bernese Mountain Dog record books show her as "Backcountry's Seeing Stars" and she has certainly enjoyed seeing all the stars in this show!

Excerpt from the Playbill of "Living the Island Life"

Chapter Five

SUNSHINE IN DOG FORM

Growing Old

For humans there are challenges galore when we all reach a certain age. Even while some of these challenges are expected, it is still unsettling. It is the time in our lives when we have to adjust to letting go of times past when we had the energy and health to achieve our goals in life, let alone our activities of daily living.

Then one day it hits - the constant adjustments of losing physical energy, possibly dealing with declining health, and ultimately facing the reality of inevitable death.

Dylan's Bike Trailer Accommodation

Unlike humans, animals most likely don't have the ability of conception, at least with any complexity. My observations could be wrong. I'm just guessing and trying to refrain from projecting onto them. Assuming this is accurate, animals don't have the capacity to understand what's happening to them. Dylan became unable to do all the things he enjoyed such as being with people who adored him and invited him into their beds, running along side me as I rode my bicycle on the local bike path, and experiencing all the interesting sights and smells in nature, to name a few.

So I made some necessary accommodations in order to extend his time outdoors. He was still able to enjoy the bike path, just not on his own. Therefore, at the age of thirteen and one half, he was able to continue to enjoy going to the park and riding along the bike path. Sometimes, a friend would join Dylan.

Ride sharing with a friend

Time to say Goodbye

After all the comfort he gave to young and old alike, at the age of 14 and 1/4 years on the planet with us, Dylan died.

Parting was gut wrenching for me, as it is for all of us who have lived so closely with someone.

After Dylan's death, I went to work as usual and busied myself in all of the necessary activities when my administrative assistant popped her head in my office to tell me that the president of the North Middlesex

Beloved service dog, Dylan, dies

which were sponsored by the Greater Lowell Hospice and Visiting Nurses as well as the American Cancer Society. When he was four years old Dylan joined the American Red Cross disaster services team to provide comfort therapy to those in unexpected tragic circumstance.

In June 2000 Dylan was officially appointed Town Hall Dog by the Ashby Board of Selectmen, a post he had been covering since July 1997. Over the 10 years he served in this position he performed such duties as welcoming people, retrieving the mail from the post office, delivering interoffice messages and assisting in the Town Clerk's office. In 2003 he received a special citation from the House of Representatives of the Commonwealth of Massachusetts.

Dylan's hobbies included acting in community theatre, with performances as "Sandy" from the Broadway musical *Annie* and "Snoopy" from *You're a Good Man, Charlie Brown*. He received a standing ovation for his rendition of "The Dog Bone Blues" in Ashby's revue *Looking at Life with a Touch of Whimcy*.

Dylan, as left, takes his place on the choir loft during services at the Winchendon Unitarian Universalist Church

ASHBY — Well known and loved registered service dog, Dylan, died Saturday, May 26, after a prolonged illness. Throughout his 14 1/2 years Dylan brought light and love to many people, young and old, and animals of several species.

The golden retriever was born on Feb. 20, 1993 in Ashburnham and went to live with Linda Sanders, current town administrator of Ashby, in April of that year. At the age of seven months Dylan began work as a therapy dog at Health Alliance's The Highlands in Fitchburg and Quabbin Valley Health Care in Athol. He loyally attended the patients and residents in those two facilities for a decade until he retired in September 2003 due to respiratory problems.

Dylan visited the Cedar Street Retirement Home and also served at the Clinton Hospital mental health department and Lowell General Hospital in special children's bereavement programs

He also enjoyed spending time in the outdoors with his cat and dog friends. In recent years, Dylan was warmly embraced as a member of the Winchendon Unitarian Universalist Church congregation and choir.

Dylan leaves his main person, Linda Sanders of Winchendon, and innumerable others who have established loving relationships with him over the years. Friends of Dylan in several communities have requested that a memorial service be held in his honor. Details of a July memorial service for Dylan will be announced when available.

Donations in memory of Dylan may be made to the Katie Fund at Canterbury Tales Veterinary Clinic, 40 Main Street, Ware, MA, 02571. The Katie Fund supports veterinary services for low income and rescued animals.

"Winchendon Courier" on June 13, 2007

Regional Red Cross was on the phone and wanted to know when Dylan's memorial service will be because she wanted to "say a few words" at it. What? She does remember that he was a dog, doesn't she? I had planned to grieve quietly by myself, but as the word of Dylan's death hit the newspapers, the demand to acknowledge his life and "say goodbye" flooded in from all directions. I hesitantly gave in, reminding myself that he was important to many others and was not just a family pet.

Dylan Was Compassionate

By Mary-Flora Hale

My first and only real encounter with Dylan was three years ago at Allen Phillips' funeral. Allen was Ashby's long time Dog Officer and Animal Control Officer, and Dylan came to know, and loved, Allen because of his very frequent visits to the Ashby Town Hall.

On that September mid-morning Dylan attended Allen's service at the Ashby Congregational Church. As he walked down the aisle he carried a bouquet of freshly cut flowers, very gently in his mouth, and then laid himself down in front of the casket as if he were an honor guard.

Bertha, Allen's wife of 62 years, was sitting in the front pew with tears quietly rolling down her cheeks. Dylan in a gentle and understanding way got up, still holding the flowers in his mouth, and walked over to Bertha. He placed his head on her lap and gave her the bouquet. After a moment or two he then laid down at her side, where he stayed until I returned from "remembering Allen."

I was unable to control my emotions and Dylan knew I needed a shoulder to cry on. He came over to me, put his head on my lap and licked my hand and looked at me with compassion and a sad smile in his eyes - as if to reassure me that he knew Allen was at peace and everything would be alright.

After another few moments with me he must have felt I was going to be okay, and he left me to once again take up his post in front of the casket. There he stayed until the service was over and everyone had left the church.

Again, two years ago I had contact with Dylan. This time it was in conjunction with his plea for help to defray the medical expenses for Joey, the Ashby dog that had been mistreated and was on the verge of starvation.

He truly was a ministry dog. He had unconditional love for his fellow creatures ... both two and four legged. Many will miss him - as I do now.

"Trilogy" Obituary on June 2, 2007

Dylan mourned as town loses official dog

Retriever had many duties

By M. Elizabeth Roman
TELEGRAM & GAZETTE STAFF

ASHBY—The 14-year-old was an actor, a venerated town official and a companion for the sick and elderly for most of his life.

But after a long illness, Dylan, a golden retriever, died Saturday. He left a unique legacy that officials say will not be forgotten.

Dylan was appointed Town Hall Dog by the Ashby Board of Selectmen in 2000. The only dog ever named to the post, he follows a rare tradition set by Bum, a Saint Bernard and spaniel mix that became the official city dog of San Diego in the late 1800s. Rockford, Ala., population 450, lost its official town dog, Fred, in 2002.

Sally Bauman, chairman of the Ashby Board of Library Trustees, was well acquainted with Dylan's duties at Town Hall.

"He has always been an ever-present source of delight," Mrs. Bauman said. "He was a very unusual dog in that he just seemed to understand what people were thinking. He seemed to know when to interact and when to sit back."

Dylan at a groundbreaking ceremony in a photo provided by the town.

His duties included welcoming visitors, retrieving the mail from the post office, delivering interoffice messages and assisting in the town clerk's office. He also went to all the town meetings and selectmen's meetings.

"And sometimes at selectman's meetings, just when you might feel like sighing to yourself because you think, 'Oh give me a break,' just at the moment, you would hear Dylan let out a sigh," Mrs. Bauman said. "It was just what everyone was feeling."

Selectman Geoffrey Woollacott said he only got to know the dog in the last year.

"It was a very good dog. He was a fixture," Mr. Wollacott said. "He would just come up and stick his head on your lap."

Owner Linda Sanders, the Ashby town administrator, enlisted Dylan's people-expertise at nursing homes starting in 1993 when he was 7 months old. For 10 years he brought cheer and companionship to the

ASHBY

residents of The Highlands in Fitchburg and Quabbin Valley Health Care in Athol.

He visited Cedar Street Retirement Home and served at the Clinton Hospital mental health department. Dylan also brought his services to the children's bereavement program at Lowell General Hospital. When he was 4 years old Dylan joined the American Red Cross' disaster services team to provide comfort therapy to those in tragic circumstance.

When he retired from his work at The Highlands in 2003, he was greeted by state and local officials.

Nearly 60 residents of The Highlands attended Dylan's retirement party. Then state Rep. Brian Knuuttila, D-Gardner, presented the dog with a proclamation from the state House of Representatives, honoring his service.

Dylan also acted in community theater, performing as Sandy in the musical "Annie" and Snoopy from "You're a Good Man Charlie Brown."

"Everyone was so impressed," Mrs. Bauman said of Dylan's performance in the theater. "He was the only dog I ever knew that got a standing ovation."

"Telegram & Gazette" on May 30, 2007

So I agreed to a service for Dylan at the beautiful Cathedral in the Pines in Rindge, New Hampshire.

I was told that there were around 100 people in attendance. It didn't look like that many to me, but I wasn't paying much attention to numbers.

Part of the Congregation at the Cathedral in the Pines

Dylan touched so many and had a wide reaching impact.

Program Cover

Program Back

Two clergy people presided, the organist played, the choir sang, and two dogs led the recession.

Summary

Frequently, Dylan and I were commended for our selfless commitment to helping others. I attempted to correct the impression that we were a couple of "do-gooders" who were in it for the rewards and recognition. What we were here for was to answer a commitment to ease the suffering of others in any way they needed. Preferably anonymously, although that was impossible when our presence was required.

"I'm not sunshine, Betty. I'm your best friend, Dylan. We are just here together, so deal the cards."

Betty, the lady pictured here and on the cover above was 101-years-old at the time of this visit. Dylan became her very close friend, which may be why she equated his presence in her life with sunshine.

I will never forget the day when we approached Betty's hospital room for Dylan's and Betty's customary visit and found her family standing around her bed. They greeted us by coming out of her room to tell me what was happening. I apologized for disturbing them. Her daughter, an elderly person herself, said "No, please don't go. Mother has been in a coma since late last night and is not expected to make it through the day, but if you don't mind bringing Dylan in by her bed, I'm sure she would appreciate it if she happens to be aware of anything at all."

Of course, I agreed. We pulled up a chair very close so Dylan could sit next to her. He put his head on the bed and his paw next to her hand and wouldn't move for what seemed like several hours. I'm really not sure how long it was. I know that family members, doctors, and nurses came in and out several times. At one point, I left the room to tell the other patients who expected to see Dylan that he wouldn't be making his usual rounds that day. When I returned to Betty's room, her son met me in the hall, somewhat lighter, which I interpreted as excitement. He told me that his mother actually moved her hand! He didn't know whether that meant that she was coming out of the coma or not, so I went into the room and found Betty's hand over Dylan's paw. As used to as I was at witnessing some incredibly positive reactions to Dylan, I was surprised at this one.

Dylan was not going to budge so we hoisted him up in the bed to snuggle with his good friend. I left to see other people and kept coming back to see if Dylan was ready to leave. I remember it was about 7:30 that evening when I came back to the room and found Dylan licking Betty's face. He was ready to leave then. I asked Betty's son if someone would let me know if she passed away during that night. Of course they would.

I didn't get a phone call that night, so I called the hospital to check on the situation the next morning. The nurse said that Betty had pulled through the night and woke up in the morning very hungry. I asked if she wanted me to bring Dylan in to see her. The nurse said she would ask when she made her rounds. When she called me back later she told me that Betty said that wouldn't be necessary because he had already been in and slept with her. I don't know whether to attribute Betty's recovery to Dylan's help or not because sometimes people come out of comas when there is no expectation that they will. All I know is that Dylan knew when he could leave and Betty woke up hungry.

Betty used to regularly say to Dylan: "You and the sunshine, Dylan, are the two greatest lights in my life." I imagined his response to be, "I'm just here *with* you. It's merely devotion."

Epilogue

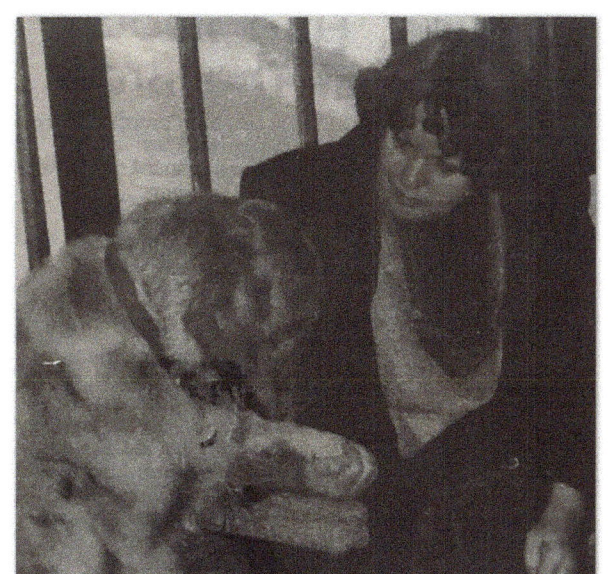

Dylan and I had a good run together. I will be forever grateful that he shared his life with me and enriched the lives of so many others.

What else is left to say?

In the Sunshine Forever Now

www.ingramcontent.com/pod-product-compliance
Lightning Source LLC
Chambersburg PA
CBHW051331120626
46547CB00016B/2489